T0207803

Boaters:
Beware of Repair Bills

Learn How to Maintain Your Own Boat
and Save Thousands of Dollars

Boaters:
Beware of Repair Bills

Learn How to Maintain Your Own Boat
and Save Thousands of Dollars

Michael Bivona, CPA

BOATERS: BEWARE OF REPAIR BILLS
LEARN HOW TO MAINTAIN YOUR OWN BOAT
AND SAVE THOUSANDS OF DOLLARS

iUniverse books may be ordered through booksellers or by contacting:

iUniverse
1663 Liberty Drive
Bloomington, IN 47403
www.iuniverse.com
844-349-9409

Because of the dynamic nature of the Internet, any web addresses or links contained in this book may have changed since publication and may no longer be valid. The views expressed in this work are solely those of the author and do not necessarily reflect the views of the publisher, and the publisher hereby disclaims any responsibility for them.

Any people depicted in stock imagery provided by Thinkstock are models, and such images are being used for illustrative purposes only. Certain stock imagery © Thinkstock.

ISBN: 978-1-5320-2448-1 (sc)
ISBN: 978-1-5320-2447-4 (e)

Library of Congress Control Number: 2017911700

Print information available on the last page.

iUniverse rev. date: 06/08/2022

Table of Contents

PREFACE—BOATERS: BEWARE OF REPAIR BILLS.
LEARN HOW TO MAINTAIN YOUR OWN BOAT
AND SAVE THOUSANDS OF DOLLARS

This topic has been stewing in the back of my mind for a long time. I have been a boat owner for over forty years and have experienced almost every conceivable boat repair possible, from minor tune-ups to rebuilding engines. As I recall, there were very few times when I was pleased with the cost of the repair work done.

So, why have I now decided to write about this topic? Well, over the years, I have known many boat owners who have given up boating because it had become too expensive, mainly due to exorbitant repair bills and the unpleasantness of trying to reason with repair shops as to the cost of their services. Recently, two of my dear friends have become members of the "former boaters' club." They had been boating for over thirty years, and giving up boating was a traumatic experience for them and their families. As they had owned their most recent boats for many years, the cost of repairs, due to wear-and-tear and regular maintenance, became too much for them to handle financially, so they decided to give up their prized possessions and sold their babies.

In my forty-plus years of boating, I have owned four boats in Brooklyn and Long Island, NY. They were an 18' Crestliner runabout, *Big One*. A 28' Chris Craft Cabin Cruiser, *Alice B.* A 35' Chris Craft Double Cabin, *Mikara III,* and my current boat, a 42'

Chris Craft Catalina, *Mikara*, which I purchased new and have been happily enjoying with family and friends for almost thirty years. The name of our boat, *Mikara*, came from the first three letters of my name, Mike, and the last three letter of Barbara's name.

A photo of the beauty follows:

We have docked our boats permanently at five marinas and have visited over thirty others in our voyages. I'm fortunate that, through the years, I was able to perform a good deal of the boat maintenance and minor repairs myself, with the help of my father-in-law, Captain Charlie. But, there have been times in our travels that I was unable to handle various repairs and, out of necessity, had to rely on whatever service people were available to get my boats back in safe running order.

As I have been in boating for many years, I'm sure that my experience in maintaining a boat might be of interest to boaters and may even help them save money on the repairs and maintenance of their crafts. It's my hope that this will result in prolonging their boating experiences by keeping costs at a reasonable and tolerable financial level.

I estimate that over my forty-plus years of boating, in which I did as much of the work necessary to keep my boats safe and sound, I've saved well over a $150,000 (see Chapter Eight—Summary of Savings.) In addition to that enormous savings, by doing small chores like keeping oil, engine water, steering fluid, battery levels, and transmission levels at their correct heights and constantly checking for loose screws, bolts, wires, motor mounts, and inboard zinc stability to reduce the possibility of electrolysis, and keeping a close watch on my preventive maintenance list, I would venture to say that I saved an additional $50,000 and, without a doubt, avoided many unhappy breakdowns.

CHAPTER ONE

Marinas' Pricing Practices

There was a time that boat service departments' charges were based on the qualifications of its mechanics; for instance, work done by a licensed first rate mechanic doing repair work would be charged at their highest rate, work by his assistant would be charged at a lower rate, and work by a trainee would be charged at an even lesser rate. But recently, at many marinas, the upper rate is being applied to all boat repairs and maintenance. Rates are also very location sensitive. Charges in Florida and, let's say, Connecticut are usually lower than in New York. Currently, the highest rate where I'm located in New York is $125 an hour, plus environmental charges and NY State Sales Tax, which brings the figure to almost $140 an hour. In addition to the labor costs, the price of parts can be double and sometimes triple the price paid by a consumer at a marine store. As we can see by doing some arithmetic, it's imperative that skippers do as much work on their boats as possible. It could mean the difference as to whether staying in boating happily and financially can be accomplished realistically.

To give you some insight into the practice of many marina operations, some marinas pay their managers an over-ride percentage from the cost of boat repairs and services. It's these same managers, in many cases, that are responsible for preparing bills for boaters' charges. I'm a retired Certified Public Accountant (CPA), and when I was active in the profession, one of the cardinal rules for proper internal control—which was always scrutinized in a business when examining a company's financial records—was the separation of an employee's duties that might be considered a conflict of interest, such as a bookkeeper being responsible for authorizing vendors' payments and for paying their invoices. I mention this so that boaters should be aware that their bills for repairs and maintenance should be examined and questioned in detail. As a matter of fact, when work is required, **a written estimate should be requested from service departments,** circumstances permitting, so that a decision can be made, in advance, whether to have the work done. This will allow a boater time to decide if and where the work should be performed at the most advantageous price.

I think marinas that have a manager's over-ride policy based on repair income should consider having repair bills calculated by the administrative staff to reduce the temptation of overbilling.

As boaters, we know that, in most instances, time is of the essence when having a boat ready for safe use, since the boating seasons in most states, like New York and Connecticut, are only a few months of the year. When there is an emergency, most service departments will not quote a dollar amount for a job, but will base their work on time and materials. **Beware:** always insist on an estimate, unless there is extensive damage to your boat, such as a collision or hitting unforeseen objects in the water. Fortunately, most of these disasters are covered by a boat owner's insurance. Regardless, get a ballpark figure and, time allowing, price the work elsewhere. Even if the damage is covered by insurance, staying apprised as to the quality of repairs should always be uppermost in a boat owner's mind. If a skipper does not understand the mechanics of the work being done on his boat, then having a knowledgeable friend or even hiring a professional to assess the quality of the service being performed should be seriously considered.

CHAPTER TWO

From Pencil Pusher to Part-Time Mechanic

An important observation that I made over the years is that when there was an error in a service department's billing for my boats, the errors were **never**—and I say forty-plus years of **never**—in my favor. **So, let the boater beware.** Another lesson I learned the hard way was never to give *carte blanche* to a service department by saying, "Do whatever you think is necessary," without getting a written estimate; those words can result in a costly mistake. A good example is when I first purchased *Mikara*. It had a 12-gallon fresh hot water tank, which my wife thought was too small for our growing family, especially since the boat had a small bathtub that Barbara was planning on using regularly. I told the service department where I bought her (the boat not my wife) to install a larger 20-gallon tank. I asked the manager what the tank would cost; he said about $400. I told him to do whatever was necessary to install a replacement, figuring the total cost would be double the price of the unit. Well, I received a $2,500 bill for the installation, which I immediately questioned. I was told that the smaller hot water tank was a stand-alone one and only could be heated when the boat was connected to shore power. So, he thought it would be a nice feature to have the new tank attached to the left engine, so that when the boat was running it would automatically heat the water in the tank. I angrily said, "Shouldn't you have called me to let me know what you were doing in addition to what I requested and let me make the decision as to whether I wanted to spend so much dough?" To make a long story short, we settled on $2,000, which was still much more than I had anticipated spending.

You may ask: what was a CPA was doing working in the bilge of his boats doing minor repairs and much of the necessary maintenance required to keep his boats shipshape? Well, my evolution to adding a part-time mechanic's title to my professional accounting one began when I kept my 28' Chris Craft, *Alice B*, in a Lindenhurst, Long Island marina. In addition to winter storage, I had their service department winterize my boat. Being a relatively new large boat owner, I thought it would be a good idea to check my boat after it was serviced and in drydock, especially being that we were getting extremely cold weather that winter. My father-in-law, Charlie, who was an experienced boater and a fair mechanic, came along to make sure I didn't get into any trouble while inspecting *Alice B*.

We climbed onto her and right away noticed two things that were wrong: the winter cover had a baseball-sized hole on the top and snow was accumulating on the aft deck and my engine hatch was open. I had a 250hp Chris Craft single-screw, salt-water–cooled engine that was located below the aft deck; it too had evidence of being wet. Even though I was a somewhat inexperienced boater, I realized that whoever had serviced my boat had been extremely careless. Upon further inspection, we found that the forward drain plug was not removed and water was accumulating in the bilge. I thought, *Imagine if that condition remained throughout the winter. I don't know what horror we would have found on my boat in the spring.* Of course, I immediately removed the front plug so that any water in the bilge would drain out of the boat. Captain Charlie decided to check to see if antifreeze was put in the engine. He checked the radiator; it had green fluid indicating that antifreeze was used. He then removed the drain plug from the engine and salt water came out. The mechanic evidently had drained some of the water, but not all, and then put antifreeze in the radiator. Charlie said that it could have caused a crack in the engine, which would have cost thousands of dollars to replace. He then removed one of the spark plugs, which, if the engine were properly fogged for storage, should have had evidence of oil residue. It did not.

Needless to say, we confronted the yard manager and told him what we had found. He couldn't understand how one of his men could do such irresponsible work and said that he was going to fire that person. He also told us to wait while he got a different mechanic to fix the sloppy work. In the back of my mind, I said to myself, *Odd. I wonder how much money they saved and how much more they would have earned in the spring when the resulting repairs from their carelessness had to be done, all at my expense and inconvenience?* He put his mechanic to work while the Captain and I went for a long lunch that included a couple of drinks to take the edge off the unpleasant and unfathomable experience. Of course, when we returned, we didn't waste any time checking the mechanic's work to make sure that it was done properly. **Here is an example where the resultant exorbitant charges, due to their carelessness, could have put me out of boating**. In the spring, if there had been extensive damage to *Alice B* and the costs of repairing her had been unreasonable, I probably would have given up boating and missed out on all the wonderful years that my family and friends, enjoyed on my boats.

There is an old saying: "Once I'm fooled, shame on you; twice fooled, shame on me." I had no intention of having that kind of experience repeat itself. Barbara and I were members of the United States Power Squadron (USPS), and one of their courses was on boat repairs and maintenance. I didn't have time to attend that night course at St. Francis College in Brooklyn, NY, as I was busy raising a family and starting my own accounting practice, but I was able to get a copy of their course's instruction manual. With the manual and Captain Charlie's patience, I began what would become a lifetime, part-time hobby. I was determined to learn and apply what I had learned to becoming as self-sufficient as my ability and time would allow.

I would strongly advise boaters to become members of the USPS, for the safety and social aspects of the organization and for the many courses that they have available that can make the life of a boater safer, more pleasant, and less costly. For those who are not familiar with the organization, attached is a brief description of its intent and purpose by *Wikipedia, the free encyclopedia:*

United States Power Squadrons

From Wikipedia, the free encyclopedia

The **United States Power Squadrons (USPS)** is a non-profit educational organization, founded in 1914, whose mission is to improve maritime safety and enjoyability through classes in seamanship, navigation, and other related subjects. The USPS comprises approximately 45,000 members organized into 450 squadrons across the United States and in some US territories. It is the largest U.S. non-profit boating organization and has been honored by three U.S. presidents for its civic contributions. Its official publication is *The Ensign* magazine.

There are many educational opportunities available within the United States Power Squadrons. USPS offers courses that teach basic knowledge (http://www.usps.org/e_stuff/Basic.html) necessary to operate boats safely and legally. The basic course meets the requirements set forth by NASBLA (http://www.nasbla.org/). The United States Power Squadrons offer courses in advanced navigation using modern equipment such as GPS and Radar. Courses are even offered in celestial navigation. USPS also teaches advanced courses in Weather, Marine Engine Maintenance, Marine Electronic and Electrical Systems, Sail, and Cruise Planning.

One critical activity of the United States Power Squadrons is Vessel Safety Check (http://safetyseal.net/). During a Vessel Safety Check, a qualified USPS Vessel Examiner will board vessels (with permission) and check for the presence and condition of various pieces of equipment required by federal and state laws for the safe operation of that particular vessel. A vessel safety check is provided at no charge and is not a law enforcement boarding. If the boat carries the proper equipment, a sticker will be awarded to display on the vessel. If a boat does not pass the inspection, the USPS informs the owners, but does not report its findings to any law enforcement or government agency.

A parallel organization operates in Canada under the name **Canadian Power and Sail Squadrons (CPS)** in English and **Escadrilles canadiennes de plaisance (ECP)** in French. It was founded as an offshoot of USPS in 1938.

United States Power Squadrons Ensign

The USPS ensign features a red canton with 13 white stars around a fouled (entangled or twisted) anchor. The body of the flag contains 13 vertical blue and white stripes. This flag was designed by Roger Upton and Charles F. Chapman for the United States Power Squadrons, and by 1915, the flag was officially adopted by the organization. The design and other specifications of this ensign are described in the USPS bylaws and also in the operations manual.

USPS Ensign (Flag)

The Engine Maintenance Manual Stated:

Every skipper needs to understand the fundamentals of gas and diesel engines to perform basic maintenance and diagnose problems while under way. Learn about transmissions, propellers, and steering. Get the knowledge you need to keep your boat in tiptop shape.

What's Included?

- Basics of engine layout and operation for gasoline inboards, outboards, and diesels
- Basic mechanical systems, such as drive systems (propellers), steering, and engine controls
- Repairs that do-it-yourselfers can perform
- Diagnose problems that might be beyond your ability to fix
- How to share information with your mechanic so that the right repairs get performed

Engine maintenance can be taught in ten two-hour sessions, including time for review and the multiple choice, closed book exam.

It wasn't easy for a pencil-pusher like myself to absorb much of the technical information required to become familiar with the mechanics of a boat, but with the help of Captain Charlie and hands-on experience, I slowly began learning the names of the different parts of my boat and engine. I couldn't believe that I was starting to get the hang of repairing minor problems, such as fixing hose leaks, tightening screws and motor mounts, putting oil in the engine, checking the radiator for the proper water level, checking the transmission fluid, changing belts, and most importantly, checking battery fluid levels. In those days, all batteries had to be checked for proper fluid levels; today, many batteries are enclosed and self-sufficient and don't require that safety procedure. And, believe it or not, with Captain Charlie's help, I was able to winterize *Alice B* when the following boating season ended, including fogging the engine.

Winter Storage

Here's how we started winterizing *Alice B*. We filled the gas tank after putting Store & Start into it, to protect the gas from breaking down and to restrict the amount of condensation that could accumulate in the tank over the winter. Next, we ran the engine until it was hot. Then we turned the engine off and drained the oil through the oil dipstick receptacle with a portable DC suction motor, which we attached to one of the batteries. In about twenty minutes, all the oil from the engine was in a plastic container for recycling. I then replaced the oil filter, using a wrench that the Captain supplied. We poured fresh oil into the engine, and a job that would have cost a couple of hundred bucks to have done by a service department—plus parts, environmental charges, and sales tax—was completed by us in a short amount of time, properly. As my future boats had two engines and a generator, of course the savings tripled. I figured that, over the course of 40 years, I saved over $15,000 by changing the oil and filters myself.

Next, the Captain had me purchase a hose plumbing fitting to install on the top of the salt water intake strainer so we could flush out the engine with fresh water. This meant that we wouldn't have to disconnect the stiff intake hose, which he said could be a difficult getting off and replacing without being damaged. It might sound complicated, but as he was a plumber, attaching the hose fitting to the top of the intake strainer was a piece of cake for him. Below is what one of the four fittings on my 42' Chris Craft looks like. In addition to the starboard engine fitting, there is also one for the port engine, generator, and air conditioning system:

We attached our dockside fresh water hose to the fitting, opened the water valve, and ran the engine for fifteen minutes, so we could wash away some of the salt water and residue in the system. The bonus was that it also set up the engine to be winterized with antifreeze by connecting a washing machine hose, which has two female connections, to the new fitting. After putting three gallons of antifreeze in a bucket, we detached the fresh water dockside hose from the washing machine hose, put the free end of the washing machine hose into the bucket of anti-freeze, and *Voila*, the engine was winterized. We had saved another couple of hundred bucks, plus-plus-plus.

The satisfaction of knowing that these two simple procedures were done properly served me for the next forty years, as I continued using them on my single and twin screw engines. A further bonus was that my next boats had generators and air conditioners, which I winterized in the same manner, in a short period of time, without having to pay expensive labor and parts charges plus fees and taxes. When I purchased my next two beauties, I had hose plumbing fittings installed on the top of the intake strainers of the engines, generators, and air conditioner systems. Over the course of the more than forty years that I owned single and twin screw boats, I figured I saved easily over $20,000 by performing the work myself.

Our next challenge was to winterize the boat's fresh water system. We emptied the tank and then poured four gallons of nontoxic antifreeze into it. We then ran the sinks and shower water until they turned pink. This method became very useful on my larger boats, as they had ice makers and several intake fittings on the decks that were not easy to protect from freezing in the cold winter months in our area. On these boats, I would run the icemaker, using the tank system, until it produced pink ice cubes. Running the antifreeze through the sinks and outside hose fittings completed the job. Again, at least a few hundred bucks, plus-plus-plus, was saved. Over my years of boating, I figured I saved in excess of $15,000 using this method. Many boaters prefer forcing air throughout their fresh water systems to remove water from their lines, but some of my friends that used this method were welcomed by broken hoses in the spring.

While we were in the winterizing mood, Charlie thought it would be a perfect time to clean the seawater intake strainer and stainless steel (s/s) filter basket. I couldn't believe how simple the procedure was. At a marine store, he purchased a multipurpose wrench that is used to open outside stainless steel gas caps, fresh water intake caps, and intake sea strainer caps. Using the part of the wrench that fitted the strainer cap and applying a little muscle, the cap was easily unscrewed. After removing and cleaning the s/s basket and the inside of the intake strainer with a small brush, we returned the basket and cap to their original resting places and congratulated ourselves on how easy the job was. It was also important, when in dry dock, to open the seacock to drain any salt water that remained in the lower hose to prevent it from freezing. *Alice B* was a single screw, so that ended that procedure in a short time. My future larger boats took more time as they had twin engines, generators, and air conditioning units, all totaling four sea water intake strainers and s/s baskets. But the procedure was the same and doing it saved me a significant amount of money. Recently, I couldn't get the strainer caps off as my old hands no longer had the strength, so I had my marina clean the strainers; the charge was $500-plus. I figured, conservatively, that in the years that I was able to perform the cleaning, I saved well over $15,000.

While I was getting comfortable in the bilge, Captain Charlie suggested that we clean the flame arrester that was attached to the top of the carburetor. We detached the flame arrester from the carb and cleaned it with a Gum-Out Spray. Within seconds, the bucket was filled with black residue and the flame arrester was sparkling clean, as if it were brand new. Again, on my future boats, I used the same procedure, but there would be three flame arresters to clean from two engines and a generator. I chuckled when he removed a plastic shower cap from his pocket and put it around the flame arrester and carburetor. He said, "To keep moisture out of the carb during the winter months." This is a procedure that is often overlooked by service departments, so it's important that skippers check the flame arresters on their engines and generators and keep them sparkling clean to reduce possible carburetor problems during the boating season.

I was sure that our work was done, but the Captain had some other things he thought we should take care of to save more bucks. He bought a tube of yellow grease and had me apply some to the throttle and shift cables to protect them from getting damaged and to keep them in good working condition in the next boating season. He also had me put some of the yellow stuff on the moving part of the carb and the gear-shift slides. For sure, I thought that my education had come to an end, but he had some other projects in mind while I was still holding the tube of grease. He opened the aft hatch, pointed to the rudder shaft, and said, "Get in there and spread some of that stuff around the exposed part of the steering cable." It was easy enough, so I did as I was told, while he turned the steering wheel to cover the sliding part of the cable. He also did the same with the throttle and gear shift. Again, this is also a procedure often overlooked by many service departments and could cost boaters mucho bucks when the systems fail to perform properly due to jamming or corrosion.

I said, Okay, Charlie, I guess that just about finishes our day's work. He said, "I don't think so."

He purchased a set of screwdrivers and wrenches and told me to tighten all the screws, nuts, and bolts that I could reach. The whole process took about fifteen minutes, and I was surprised at how many were loose and needed tightening—a few actually needed a turn or two. Again, I thought I was through for the day, when Charlie handed me a can of marine oil spray and told me to hit all the wires that were attached to screws, in addition to the ball lever on the gas valves and intake strainer. He then turned the battery switch off and told me to remove the battery cables and polish the posts and inside the cable connections with a metal battery post-brush that he supplied: He said, "You'll know when you're finished when the posts and the inside of the cables are shining."

When I achieved the shiny test, he handed me a tube of petroleum jelly and told me to put a light coat on the terminals before attaching the cables and a similar amount on the top of posts and cables to protect them from the harmful moisture that is so prevalent in a bilge and has caused many boats not to start due to corrosion developing on the cables and terminals. I have used the same procedure annually on all my boats since then and have never had an engine fail due to that condition. There are other products that are in use that can serve the same purpose. Regardless of a boater's preference, battery cables should be checked often to determine that corrosion doesn't exist, and annually cleaned and protected with a coating of an anti-corrosion product. It should always be kept in mind that the battery switch and battery charger should be in the off position when working on the batteries, or near them, to prevent any unnecessary sparks or short circuits in the bilge.

Many of my boating friends have experienced unhappy days when screws and bolts became loose or corroded battery cables stopped their boats from operating properly. In addition to the expense of having their boats towed and repaired, **the embarrassing part for them** was to find that the problems could have been easily avoided with a little personal boat maintenance of the turn of a screw or a five-minute post and cable polishing. Needless to say, I used the same procedures on my larger boats, which had many more batteries to service, and I can say that I never had a failure due to lose screws, bolts, or corroded battery cables.

A procedure that I would use every season came about after I had a near disaster, when 10 gallons of gas spilled into my bilge over the winter because of a defective fuel pump check valve. When I boarded my 42' Chris Craft in the spring, the gas fumes almost knocked me over. I immediately contacted the service department in my marina and had a mechanic come down to investigate the cause. The first thing he did was close the gas shut-off valves. He then determined that I had gas in my bilge and that my boat had to be towed out of harm's way to a nearby mooring. He mixed a stabilizing solution into the bilge and then slowly towed me to a safer location with his work boat. After tying up, I was given a plastic hand pump and two five gallon drums for safely removing, I hoped, the diluted gas from the bilge. He left me by my lonesome to fend for myself, which was one of the scariest moments of my life.

We already had opened all the windows and hatches, so there was plenty of air in the boat. I then—very slowly—began pumping the gas from the bilge into the five gallon cans, all the while praying that the fumes wouldn't ignite and send me to **a dumb boater's heaven**. After about two hours, the gas was displaced and I began scrubbing down the bilge with soap and fresh water from my water tank. When I finished, I called the service department to tow me back to my slip. I thought that was the end of the story, but it was not. Gas had gotten into the crankcase oil and had to be removed. This was done by removing the oil plug at the bottom of the crankcase and replacing the contaminated oil. I was told to drain and change the oil three times, which I did. When I finished, the mechanic told me that he would have to replace the fuel pump and rebuild the carburetor. I preferred having a new carburetor and fuel pump installed on both engines, just to play it safe. In a couple of days, the job was completed and my boat was again shipshape and ready for cruising. Or so you would think.

When I inspected the replaced fuel pumps, that's when I noticed that the small see-thru hoses attached to the pumps were black from 15 years of use. I called the mechanic responsible for the installation and asked, *Why were the 8" hoses not replaced?* He checked his work order and said that it didn't indicate that they should be replaced.

Talk about getting pissed. I lost my temper and said, *How could you install new fuel pumps and put 15-year-old brittle and dirty hoses back on them?*

I reported the incident to the service manager; he apologized for the sloppy work and said that they were in the process of firing the mechanic for similar complaints they had received from other captains. The moral of that story, as with all repair work, is: check, check, and check work that is done on your boats to make sure it's done properly; it could save your life. If not able to do so, ask a capable friend to inspect the work for you.

That event recalls a story of a friend's 40' Silverton Double Cabin that this year (2016) blew up, putting a hole in the side of his boat and sending three mechanics to the hospital, one in critical condition. The owner of the boat was unable to leave Florida and return to his craft in New York, where he has been boating for over thirty years. He decided to have his boat put in storage at a local marina until he could resume boating. He didn't have an opportunity to inspect the boat and, one way or another, she developed a gas leak while in drydock. As I heard the story from him, the gas fumes were detected and three mechanics boarded the boat to restore it to a safe condition. As the story goes, the gas was mingled with water in the bilge, so they decided to pump both the water and gas from the boat at the same time—not as I did with a plastic hand pump, but with an electric one. To make a long story short, the spark from the electric pump evidently ignited the fumes and blew the boat apart, injuring the three men. Certainly, it was a most unfortunate accident that has resulted in several lawsuits between the boat owner, the storage facility, and the injured men.

Of course, the lesson I luckily learned before a major disaster, such as my friend had, was to **close all gas valves when storing my boat for the winter.** My 42' Chris Craft has three gas tanks and three fuel pumps, which increase the possibility of the same thing happening to my boat when she is in drydock. So, when

I do my last inspection after winterizing my engines, I turn the gas valves off, one by one, and feel a sigh of relief that my unfortunate experience will not repeat itself.

A related story comes to mind of another friend who was under the impression that when his boat was put in winter storage that it was **not necessary** for him to continue his insurance coverage because the marina's insurance would cover his boat if there was a destructive event. **What a mistake it is to suspend insurance coverage.** Winter storage and all other seasonal contracts should be read carefully, and it should be duly noted that marinas require all boat owners to have their own insurance, not only to cover their boats, but to cover any damage to the marina and to other property caused by their boats. A certificate of insurance is usually requested by marinas as evidence of proper insurance coverage. It is also interesting to note that, regardless of the cause of any damage to your boat, it is your insurance that is the most reliable source of recovery. Another friend also had an incident in which his boat escaped with little damage when several boats alongside his caught fire and burned to the water level. Talk about luck: he only had singed plastic curtain damage, whereas the four boats directly on his port side were destroyed. The lawsuits and finger pointing are still going on between the owners of the damaged boats and the marina.

Springtime and Back to *Alice B*

I would like to mention that back when I worked on my 28' boat, there weren't as many marine supply stores as we have today. Now if I need supplies or a part, West Marine is right around the corner; their service is impeccable and their abundance of supplies almost limitless. Even when I'm cruising to Connecticut, Rhode Island, or Massachusetts, they have convenient stores near the waterfronts.

Fast forward to spring on Long Island, NY. After absorbing as much of the USPS maintenance guidebook over the winter as time allowed, I—with the help of the ever-faithful Captain—tackled tuning the engine on my 28' Chris to get her ready for summertime. First, we attached a new nontoxic hose to the boat and flushed out the anti-freeze from the fresh water system, which included flushing out the fresh water holding tank. As the boat had only one engine, we just had to concentrate on one set of plugs, a condenser, points, distributor cap—and a fresh set of spark plug wires, as the set on the boat looked frayed. My future boats had electronic ignitions that didn't require points or a condenser and were much easier to tune. But, be that as it may, we began the process of tuning *Alice B.* First, I turned on the gas valve and then made sure that the salt water intake was open and ready for use. Next, I checked the engine oil, radiator water, battery, and transmission fluid levels, which fortunately didn't require any service. Last, but not least, we cranked the engine to get her running after the long winter storage and to get the water pumps working, which discharged the nontoxic anti-freeze from the system in short order. I was surprised that after a few turns of the engine, she started with a hearty roar and lots of smoke from the exhaust. We only ran the engine for a couple of minutes and then waited until after lunch, when the engine had cooled, to begin the tune-up.

Thank God for Charlie; he had all the right tools that were necessary to perform the task. He told me that the tools—a spark plug wrench, a gapping tool (used to set the gap in the spark plugs and points), and a timing light (which times the engine properly)—were my May birthday present. The tools came in a handy box labeled "Tune-Ups for Dummies." Along with the other tools that he purchased for me in the winter, I had a useful mini-mechanics tool chest, which I put to good use when servicing my boats.

The first thing I did, under careful supervision, was replace the spark plug wires carefully, one by one, so I wouldn't cross-mix them. Then, I removed the old plugs and gapped the new ones to specification, again one by one: wire off, old plug off, new plug gapped and in, and then new wire attached firmly. Then the distributor cap came off and I removed the points and condenser. After gapping the new points to specification, I installed them, along with a condenser and a new distributor cap. Charlie then pointed to the two belts on the engine: one was attached to the water pump and the other to the alternator. He said they were not only loose but they looked frayed. So, off I went to fetch replacements. It took a bit of doing to get the old belts off, but with the Captain nearby and giving accurate instructions, I was able to replace both with new ones.

Again, I thought my work was done, but he said, "Let's not forget the gas filters."

The engine had an inboard filter and a water separator, and the carburetor had a small intake one. Finding the two new engine gas filters was easy enough, but locating an inline small gas filter took lots of research. I finally located one, and a spare, at a distant marine store in Freeport, Long Island, which was about 50 miles from where *Alice B* was resting. As usual, Charlie had the appropriate wrench to remove the gas filter housing, and in short order I replaced the three filters. On my larger boats, replacing the filters was a little more difficult as I not only had two engines and a generator to contend with, but some of the gas filters were in difficult places to reach. However, with patience and experience, I wisely replaced my gas filters annually.

We then ran the engine for a few minutes, enjoying the smooth purr coming from it and the exhaust. When we finished congratulating each other, Charlie timed the engine while I carefully watched. Over the years, by tuning my engines, including the generators, and replacing gas filters and belts, I probably saved more than $30,000.

When we finished, I treated the Captain to a lobster dinner and a bottle of his favorite red wine for being a patient teacher and for a job well done. After a couple of drinks with dinner, I told him that I thought I enjoyed working on the boat more than pushing pencils.

Smiling, he said, "Oh, I forgot about the zincs in the engine and on the rudder and shaft. We'll pick some up on the way home and replace them next week."

Replacing the zincs on the single screw boat was a piece of cake, but on my larger crafts I had to replace large zinc plates above the trim tabs, zinc balls on both shafts, and two zincs in each engine, for a total of six zincs.

CHAPTER THREE

Hull Maintenance

Painting the Bottom

Most marinas require that painting the bottom of boats be done by them, in accordance with environmental and safety rules. Two types of anti-fouling paints are popular: Hard Bottom and Ablative. When possible, I always preferred using Ablative Paint as it wears off as the boat travels through the water, reducing paint buildup on the bottom of a craft. The charge for this painting service is usually based on the size of the boat. Over the years, I've paid between three and seven hundred dollars per application. Unfortunately, many of the painters apply anti-fouling paint without protecting the salt water intakes with tape, resulting in their getting clogged. As we know, this will result in engines overheating and toilets not being able to take on the necessary water to work properly. Many a cruise has been interrupted by overheated engines and clogged heads. If a boat has one engine, then an expensive tow will be required, which could range from a couple of hundred dollars and upwards to a thousand bucks, depending on the distance that the boat must be towed. If a boat has twin engines, then returning to a port may, under safe conditions, be done on one engine by an experienced captain. In both cases, you are at the mercy of the nearest marina as to how soon the problem can be resolved and to the cost of repairs. The cost will involve being hauled out of the water and then probably replacing the water intake causing the problem. In my experience, it was rare that service people recommended that a clogged intake be cleaned by a diver or after the boat was hauled. Many boaters put on underwater gear and inspect, if the water is clear enough, the intakes and if possible, clean the unwanted buildup themselves.

When a boat is out of the water and a hauling cost has been incurred, mechanics usually suggest that the problem intake be replaced. The total cost for this service can run from several hundred dollars to a couple of thousand bucks, depending on the size of the boat. My suggestion is that, if an intake is in good condition and can be reasonably cleaned, saving a few hundred dollars would be a better choice than replacing the part. Also, trying to get some satisfaction from the marina responsible for painting the bottom causing the problem could be an alternative. If the hauling is done by the same marina, then chances of getting some relief is more likely than if it's done elsewhere; that is, if it's possible to get them to admit that they caused the problem. What I've learned to do annually, from having been a victim of this kind of carelessness on the part of painters, is to check the intakes after my boat is painted, to make sure they are not painted over. I also use an anti-fouling spray for metal, which I purchase at West Marine, to make sure that barnacles don't attach themselves to the intakes. Other areas of concern that I've found are:

- When anti-fouling paint is applied to a boat's transducers, depth sounders, fish finders, and whatever other devices are in use and have an underwater presence, they will become disabled. Again, it's necessary, before a boat is launched, that the captain inspect these items to make sure that they are clean and ready for safe use. If they are not functional after launching, then we are talking about hauling a boat and spending mucho bucks due to painters' carelessness, whether intentional or not.

- For boats that have trim-tabs, it's imperative that they be inspected to make sure that anti-fouling paint doesn't accumulate on the moving parts. The tabs should be tested while a boat is in drydock, to make sure they are operational. I once had my 35' Chris launched, and on its shake-up cruise, I found one of the tabs was jammed. She had to be hauled and the problem fixed, wasting a considerable amount of precious time and eliciting a nose-to-nose confrontation with the service people as to whose responsibility it was to make sure the tabs were operational prior to launching.

- Prior to a boat being launched after anti-fouling paint is applied, the owner should make sure that the whole bottom of the hull is painted. I had an experience in which only the part of the bottom that could be seen below the waterline from my dock was painted. I just happened to be present when my boat was being lifted and asked why the whole bottom wasn't done. The response from the marina manager was, "I saved you a lot of money." Of course, I insisted that the entire bottom be painted, as contracted, while I watched. Ever since that incident, I have inspected the bottom of my boats to make sure that all the work I contracted for was done properly.

While we are discussing the bottom of a boat, I should mention that it is wise to replace the zincs annually, to avoid electrolysis and the resultant cost of replacing parts on a boat that could be seriously damaged, such as wire connections, as well as metal breakdown and corrosion. On *Alice B*, the job was simple: I had one shaft zinc, a small zinc plate on the rudder, and an engine zinc to replace, which took all of fifteen minutes. But, on my larger boats, both shafts had zincs and large zinc plates in the back of the boats, which had to be unbolted and replaced with stainless steel bolts, nuts, and washers. Not a very clean job, but worth the effort, considering the harm that can be done to a boat from the damaging effects of electrolysis. The cost of marine zincs has gone up considerably over the years. Replacing them on the outside of my boats and the engines over the years has saved me in excess of $30,000.

Another checklist item that should be done annually is to have the service people clean the shafts, rudders, and propellers while they are working on the bottom. This will enhance the speed of a boat while underway and save *mucho dinero* in fuel costs. Again, before a boat is launched, skippers should make sure that the work is done properly.

Waxing the Hull and Superstructure

Recently, many marinas have instituted the same policy for hull waxing large boats on their property as they do for painting boat bottoms. They require that waxing should be done by them or their contractors, for environmental and safety reasons. That policy, however, doesn't usually apply to a boat's superstructure.

Upon owning my 42' Chris, I eventually found that waxing the hull became a major and, quite frankly, boring endeavor, especially since my son no longer could help with the tedious task, as he had gone into the military. So, I gladly turned the job over to the waxing experts with one special condition: that the boat get a good washing prior to any compounding and waxing. I say this because, many years ago, I witnessed an attempt to wax my 42' hull in the spring, after the winter layup, without an effort to wash her. When confronted, the polisher stated, "There's a cleaning solution in the wax, so it's really not necessary to wash the hull." I insisted that the entire boat be cleaned before I paid for the waxing. I watched while he performed the task that I requested, and I hung around to make sure that he completed the job on *Mikara* properly.

As for cleaning the superstructure, including the stainless-steel rails, bridge, hardware, and canvasses, up until a few years ago, I performed that task myself. The current cost for that job today is over $800, plus sales tax and environmental fees. The years that I performed that labor of love and the hull waxing when it was permitted, I figure that I saved over $25,000. I'm no longer able to perform the waxing and detailing, so I have it done every other year and have my boat professionally cleaned and detailed every week. I'm not concerned about saving money at this time of my life, but I must say that *Mikara* looks pristine for a 28-year-old lady.

Hull Attachments

My main concerns are the items attached to the hull that are exposed to salt water corrosion. If they are not properly maintained, there is no doubt that they will quickly corrode and cause problems and, as always, when you need them the most.

The most critical attachments are the AC dockside electrical outlets. On my boat, these are on the starboard side of the hull. Many boats, wisely, have them inside the aft deck, where there is certainly better protection from the elements. I have two 30 amp lines attached to *Mikara* that I make sure are always tight and secured with plug rings. The problem arises when underway, as salt water splashes the hull. I have built-in screw-on caps that are closed tightly to make sure salt water does not enter the sockets and possibly cause a short circuit. In the fall, when preparing my boat for winter storage, I always make sure that the outlets are clean, and I apply a light connection spray, before closing the screw-on caps tightly for the season, to protect them from the cold wet winters.

It's always a good idea in the spring to make sure that all the hull vents are clean: bilge blowers, air bilge vents, toilet blowers, washer and dryer vents, and any other goodies that sailors have for comfort or necessity. A neighbor of mine found a bird's nest in one of his vents after searching for weeks to figure out why his bilge blower was overheating and cutting out.

Another favorite pastime of mine is keeping my stainless-steel rails and other stainless fixtures polished. West Marine has a great rust remover that I use effectively. The liquid is applied easily and sets in a few minutes, and when it is removed, any unsightly or difficult rust buildups are gone. Using a companion product, I polish all my stainless steel with a wax manufactured for that purpose, and after some sweat and strain, all my shiny metal is ready to show off.

The savings for this kind of maintenance can't be measured, as replacing stainless steel parts is not only expensive, but finding the right parts may be difficult, especially as boats age or companies go out of business.

CHAPTER FOUR

Above Hull Maintenance

Although I have had many types of electronics installed on my boats, such as depth sounders, fume detectors, radios, radars, Lorans, etc., I don't recall ever having an issue with their installations that wasn't readily remedied. This was because an estimate was always obtained, and the work was usually done in accordance with the agreed upon prices and time schedules.

Canvas and Weatherboard Maintenance

My problem over the years has been with canvas work. To give an example, I recently had some aft curtains installed around the salon on *Mikara*. The curtains consisted of seven panels with see-thru plastic. I received a quote of $4,600 from a local contractor that I had used for many years. I received a second quote of $5,100 from another local canvas maker. Both prices were more than I was thinking of spending. So, I asked some of my boating buddies who they used, and they gave me the name of a company that they all seemed to be happy with. I contacted the canvas company and received a quote of $2,600. I hired them, and pleasantly, the work was installed to perfection in a timely manner. The moral of the story is: shop-shop-shop for the best price from reputable contractors, and you will save a considerable about of cash. I saved between $2,000 and $2,500 by taking my time to find the right installers.

When I tell my weatherboard story, people find it hard to believe. I have a port, starboard, and two aft weatherboards enclosing my aft salon. The port and starboard white boards measure 2 ½' by 10' by ¼". The two aft clear boards measure 2½' by 3' by ¼". Once, during a storm, the white port and aft boards were damaged. We were in Florida at the time, so I asked our marina for a quote to replace all the boards as they were 25 years old and replacing all of them would dress *Mikara* nicely. I received a quote of $6,200; this was before taxes and environment charges, which brought the price to over $7,000. I immediately called the manager of the marina and asked why the price was so high. He said that they only made acrylic boards in 4×8 foot panels, which meant that they had to add two feet to the length of the port and starboard white boards. This also meant cutting the width to 2 ½' and then attaching two feet to the length. To make sure that it would look professional, they would then have to Imron both white boards. The two clear aft boards were included in the price. Needless to say, I was shocked.

I opened my laptop and within ten minutes found a place close to where I live in Melville that would make the white acrylic boards to size for approximately $250, including drilling holes to fasten them to the stanchions of my boat. I called a local glass maker and got prices for the clear boards for an additional $250 each. I emailed the marina manager and told him that I had found a company—American Acrylic Corp. in West Babylon— that would make the white weather boards to specifications and gave him their telephone number and their prices.

I assumed that when I got back to Long Island from Florida in the spring that the boards would be installed, as two months had gone by and I hadn't heard from the manager. Well, guess what?

They were not installed. Furious, I approached the manager and asked why he hadn't gotten the job done.

He said: "We were too busy."

So, I brought my old white boards to the acrylic company and had them make the boards to size, with the exact drilling of 22 holes on each so that I could secure the boards to the stanchions and attach my aft curtains to them as well. I then had the aft clear boards made and installed all four boards myself within five hours. Total cost, including stainless steel hardware (screws, lock washers, and nuts) was under $1,200. The moral of the story is: if you can perform any maintenance or repairs on your boat, do it yourself or ask friends to help. Aside from the exorbitant quote, the aggravation of dealing with service people can be very frustrating, and in time these could be deciding factors for why boaters give up the wonderful pastime and become landlubbers. This case is a typical example of why boating has become too expensive for some people, especially if they are not capable or inclined to do repairs and maintenance on their boats themselves or with the help of friends.

An aside to my story. A fellow boater at the same marina had a weatherboard damaged during the same storm. The yard was also too busy to install a new one. When I told him my "tale of woe," he was delighted to go to the same acrylic company and have his board fabricated, including the appropriate holes for mounting and a perfect color match. It cost him a little over $300 as his board was larger than mine. With the help of a friend, he installed the weatherboard in less than a couple of hours at a fraction of the cost that the marina originally quoted. Till this day, he thanks me for the lead that saved him a lot of money and a great deal of grief. It's the repetition of this kind of unprofessional conduct of service people that have caused many boaters to pack it in.

Over the years, I found that putting some Vaseline on the inside of the canvas snaps has prolonged their use and made fastening them to the boat a lot easier than trying to place snaps that are dry. Especially in my old age, my fingers appreciate any relief they can get from the pain of trying to force snaps into place on the boat. Many products are sold for this purpose, but I still prefer the old-fashioned Vaseline.

Bridge Instrument Panel Maintenance

It goes without saying that boaters enjoy having their instrument panels and attachments kept clean and ready for use and show. I have spent many a relaxing hour polishing my instruments and chrome equipment on the bridge and taking care of the underbelly of all the various sophisticated equipment attachments and connections that are in the cabinets below the panel. With a little careful maintenance, we can go a long way in keeping them functional and ready for continuous safe boating. The storage area is one of the most crucial parts of a boat. In addition to the wiring for the instrument panel, it also contains wiring for starters, radar, depth sounders, radios, hailers, steering, GPS, and any other number of nautical necessities and boating toys. The meeting place for many of these delicate wire connections is usually housed in fuse boxes in the cabinets.

This area was brought to my attention, unfortunately, when I couldn't start my engine on my 28' Chris. The contact to my starter button was corroded and became disconnected. After that experience—which was quite easy to fix as I had a limited amount of electronics on *Alice B*—I paid close attention to the integrity of that part of the bridge. I was able to reconnect the wire to my starter button and take care of some other suspicious looking connections without too much trouble. But, on my larger boats, it was a whole different story. It wasn't as easy and it was a lot more complicated, due to the number of wires zigzagging throughout the area. The boats had two fuse boxes and all the necessary connections to the instrument panel that one expects to find on a well outfitted boat.

It's said that "Seawater and electricity have a fatal attraction love affair that can be quite dangerous," as corroded and loose wires are one of the major causes of fires and breakdowns on boats. So, annually, with lots of finesse and the battery and dockside switches in the off position, I open the fuse boxes and make sure that all the connections are tight. After that, I apply a light coating of anti-corrosion spray on the contacts. I repeat this procedure with all the other connections in the storage area. I can't even begin to estimate how much money I've saved over my forty years of boating. I'm sure that this type of preventive maintenance not only saved me money on expensive repairs, but it also kept my boats safe from any "fatal attraction" that could have disabled them. Many of my friends have had downtime from corroded wires located in the bridge cabinet area that prevented them from using their boats as often as they would have liked. I have seen boaters with wiring difficulties who had to spend much of the boating season waiting for qualified electricians to repair, or in some cases rewire, their boats. I know of two captains that gave up boating because their crafts had to be rewired because they were not only worried about the cost of doing the repairs, but they felt uneasy about owning boats that had previously had electrical problems.

Running Lights & Accessories

When busy getting boats ready for summer fun, many boaters, like myself, forget about the equipment that is on the superstructure, such as running lights, spotlights, hailers, horns, dingy davits, hose and wash down connections, outriggers, and water drains. In the spring, it only takes a couple of hours to check to see if the above items are functional, and a short amount of time to correct any that are not. As a matter of fact, I check many of these items in the fall so that I have time in the winter months to fix or replace any that are suspicious looking or not working properly. Last year, I had a problem with my hailer. I located the instruction booklet and found that the distributor was a local company. I didn't waste any time in calling them to describe the problem I had with the unit. They determined that the malfunction was with the speaker and told me to bring it in so they could examine it. I delivered the defective unit to the company, and they graciously took it and replaced it with a rebuilt one, at no charge. I'm sure I saved at least a few hundred bucks by replacing the speaker myself rather than having a technician check the problem and charge me for his time and probably the cost of a new speaker. Considering that there have been very few times that a technician has visited my boats that I wasn't charged for at least two hours of labor plus parts, I figured that I saved about $500 by researching and pursuing a remedy myself.

Another item I recently replaced was my radio antenna. My marine radio was giving me trouble with incoming calls. I contacted the radio manufacturer and explained the problem. They had me put the equipment through some tests and determined that the antenna was the cause of the malfunction. I immediately went to West Marine and purchased a replacement, which came with an installation sheet. In less than an hour, I removed the defective one and replaced it, and presto, my radio functioned perfectly. Calling a technician to determine the reason for the malfunction would have probably cost me the price of a couple of hours of labor and possibly replacement of the unit. The labor charge savings was at least $250. The cost of a new radio would probably have run $500+.

There is no doubt that just nosing around the deck hardware and equipment will detect suspicious looking rust, clogged drains, deteriorating hoses, etc., before they become unwanted headaches during the boating season.

Cabin Maintenance

AC/DC Electric Panels

Probably the most overlooked place on boats for maintenance by seamen are the AC/DC electric panels that are in their cabins. We take for granted that all we must do is press the buttons or switches and they will forever function properly. If you are one of the fortunate sailors that trades up every few years, that may be the case. But if you own a boat, as I have, for long periods of time or if you have a preowned boat, then maintaining the panels should be a priority on your checklist of things to do annually. The AC/DC panels are the heart of a boat, as they supply the electrical power that is essential for the safety and comfort of mariners. There is no doubt that the panels look complicated and intimidating, but ignoring proper maintenance can result in disaster, as incidences from corroded or shorted wires can cause lots of downtime for sailors. Without a doubt, many of the fires on boats can be traced to poor maintenance of electric panels.

We know, when we plug our shorelines in and through the appropriate switches, that presto, all the necessary AC powered machinery is ready for instant use. Refrigerators, ice makers, air conditioners, heaters, hot water heaters, lights, stereos, televisions, and a multitude of other toys that boaters are addicted to are instantly ready for use. Oh, let's not forget **battery chargers.** As we know, they keep our batteries properly charged so that we can easily start our engines, or if we decide to spend the night on the hook, we will have the same reliable use of the previously mentioned conveniences, thanks to our generators that are entirely reliant on our batteries. Let's not forget all the DC powered electronics and equipment, such as radar, GPS, horns, radios, toilets, winches, satellite, and whatever other preferred goodies sailors might seem to enjoy that are also powered by the DC electricity from our batteries and our generators. In the fall, I remove any of the above-mentioned portable equipment from the boat that is not built in, for safety from thefts and inclement winter weather. I spray all the wire connections on the bridge that remain on the boat with electrical connection spray and then wrap them in plastic baggies secured with outdoor tape.

I find that, in the spring, when the nice weather encourages me to get *Mikara* ready for an anticipated great summer, my tools seem to beckon me to unscrew the two fastenings on the AC/DC panels and look inside for any suspicious sights. Of course, before I begin, I turn off the shore and battery power so that I won't fry myself and possibly ruin my future summers. If all the wire connections seem to be intact, then I carefully place my screwdriver on the contact screws to make sure that they are tight. Where the wires are connected by the push-in method, I very gently make sure that they are tightly secured. If all goes well, then I spray, very lightly, electric contact spray on the connections to help prevent any corrosion.

While I'm inspecting the panels, if any wires are dark or look corroded, or if the push-in wires are loose and I can't easily tighten them, then I notify my marina's service department and have them send a qualified mechanic to correct any suspicious items, as I won't take a chance of screwing up the panels as they are the heart and soul of a boat.

Air Conditioners

If you're lucky to own a boat that has an air conditioner, then cleaning the filter is a very important step in keeping the unit running efficiently. So often, many of my friends lost the use of their air conditioning and had to have a mechanic check what the problem was, only to find that the air filters were dirty and caused the units to overheat. Talking about wasting money. A service person takes about 15 minutes to review with his department what the boater's problem is, another 15 minutes to reach the boat, at least 30 minutes to determine what the cause of the problems is, and another 30 to remove, clean, and replace the filter, and another 15 minutes to pack his tools and return to the shop. A service call of that nature would probably run around 2 hours, at $140 an hour, for an unnecessary charge of $280.

All a captain needs to do is remove the filter and if it's a reusable one, run it under water, let it dry, and replace. Time involved: 30 minutes; savings: $280, plus whatever cost a mechanic might **misdiagnose** the problem to be, which is not uncommon.

While discussing air conditioning systems, let's not forget the A/C pump. If it isn't oil sealed, then it requires frequent injections of oil into the motor. I put a few drops of SAE 20 into the oil ports once a month to make sure that the pump functions properly and lasts for at least seven or eight years.

Teak and Window Care

In the spring, while in the mood, my wife Barbara and I apply, with a soft cloth, a thin layer of teak cleaner oil to the teak that is in abundance throughout the inside cabin of Mikara. We also tackle cleaning the windows with cleaner polish and the tracks with silicone spray for smooth operation during the summer months.

Windlass Motor

Another item on my checklist for annual maintenance is the windlass motor and its electrical connections. On Mikara, the connections are in the forward bedroom locker. I learned the hard way about the proper maintenance of the winch after it cost me $1,500 to replace over 20 years ago. I carefully watched the mechanic remove my disabled motor and took careful instructions from him on how to maintain that expensive piece of equipment. So, every year, I turn off the DC switch for the motor and carefully make sure the heavy wires that are connected to it are tight and clean, with no evidence of corrosion. Next, I make sure the bolts connecting the wires to the motor are tight. If all is okay, I apply a light coat of electric connection spray to the whole motor and wires. While working on the winch, I go topside, where the anchor chain is located, and locate the grease fitting on the top of the winch. Using a grease gun, I inject the fittings generously. In addition to saving money on repairs and possible replacement of a motor, proper maintenance will also assure sailors dependable performance when spending time on the hook and, as many fortunate skippers have found, this has saved many a craft from going aground when engines failed and an anchor was needed to keep the boat from drifting into dangerous waters.

Replacing a winch today can run between $1,000 to $10,000, depending on the size and requirements of a boat. So, a little preventive maintenance is certainly in order and will prolong the life of that important piece of equipment.

CHAPTER FIVE

Off-Season, Winter, & Spring Maintenance Schedules

Winter Checklists

The marina that I'm currently at has an excellent procedure for having boats serviced. They use the "checklist method" for seasonal work and give written estimates for other work that is required. Attached is the schedule that I filled out for the fall of 2016:

___ OUTSIDE POWER $5.25 SQ/FT ___ OUTSIDE UNSTEPPED $4.75 SQ/FT ___ OUTSIDE MAST IN $5.75 SQ/FT
___ WET STORAGE $45/FT ___ DINGHY STORAGE (UP to 9') $250 ___ DINGHY STORAGE 9'to14' $350

ALL PRICES INCLUDE LABOR ONLY, MATERIALS WILL BE CHARGED AS USED.

HULL

___ Shrink Wrap Boat	Up to 40' $18/ft ... Over 40' $20/ft ...Flybridge + $5/ft ..... Hardtop +$3/ft	
___ Shrink Wrap Boat With Mast Stepped/Painted Hull...... Up to 40' $23/ft	Over 40' $25/ft	
___ Frame & Cover Boat (Wood frame w/canvas unstepped)		$4 SQ/ft
___ Outrigger Storage		$200.00
___ Remove Dodgers, Antennas, Outriggers & Enclosures		T&M
___ Remove Drain Plug		$15

MECHANICAL

___ Winterize one gas engine	$180
✓ Winterize two gas engines	$350
___ Winterize one diesel engine	$210
___ Winterize two diesel engines	$425
✓ Change engine oil and filter gas	$150
___ Change engine oil and filter diesel	$215
✓ Winterize generator	$175
___ Change generator oil and filter	$150
___ Change transmission fluid gas	$110
___ Change transmission fluid diesel	$145
___ Pump holding tank	$75
___ Winterize head(s)	$75each
___ Winterize water systems	T&M
___ Winterize air conditioning	$95each
___ Winterize water cooled refrigeration system	$95each
✓ Leave batteries on board, disconnect, recommended	$25each
___ Remove batteries from boat	T&M
___ Store and charge batteries	$30each
___ Store and winterize outboard auxiliary	$150(4stroke +$50)
___ Remove outboard auxiliary from boat	$50
___ Store and winterize outboard ....~100HP $150 (4 stroke + $50)............>100HP $225 (4 stroke + $50)	
___ Remove and store outdrive (Does not include installation in spring)	$200
___ Winter service outdrive (Change gear lube, sand, clean, paint, install zincs)	$350each
✓ Service seacock's	T&M
___ Remove, recondition, reinstall propeller	subcontract labor

RIGGING

___ Unstep mast under 50 ft	$11.50/ft mast length
___ Unstep mast over 50ft or triple spreader	$13.50/ft mast length
___ Store mast (with radar + $75)	$4/ft
___ Remove and store roller furler (unstepped only)	$125
___ Service roller furler	T&M
___ Service winches	T&M
___ Remove sails	T&M
___ Sail cleaning, storage, repair	subcontract labor

I have read the terms and conditions on the back of this form and the General Marina Rules and Conditions. I agree to the terms and conditions as stated. I have included 50% deposit of the storage fee. A service charge of 1.5% per month will be added to all accounts over 30 days past due. All labor and materials are subject to 1.5% environmental compliance charge. Payment is due upon receipt. Any questions must be submitted within 10 days of receipt.

Date 9/16/16   Owner's Signature _Michael Bivona_

Beware: Vessel and its contents may be sold at public auction for failure to pay charges.

As we can see from the above checklist, most of a boat's required maintenance while in storage is covered and should be attended to prior to boating season.

For sailors like myself who prefer doing a good deal of the necessary maintenance on their boats, the following is a *Winter Schedule Maintenance Checklist* that I developed over my many years of boating:

Winter Schedule Maintenance Checklist

- Fill three gas tanks and add stabilizer
- Thoroughly clean outside of boat
- Change fuel filters on engines
- Change oil and filters on engines
- Check freshwater-cooling systems coolant levels
- Drain freshwater tank and freshwater heater (f-h)
- Fill freshwater tank with nontoxic antifreeze
- Run antifreeze through freshwater system by-passing (f-h)
- Clean salt-water intakes
- Run engines and flush salt-water sides with freshwater
- Flush engines and A/C unit with antifreeze
- Fog cylinders in engines
- Cover carburetors with shower caps
- Shut-off fuel valves
- Check lead acid battery levels & polish posts and cables
- Grease all moving parts on engines
- Spray all wire connections with electric safety spray
- Clean bilge and check all pumps
- Check and spray anchor winch motor connections
- Pump out holding tank and add anti-freeze
- Clean and add anti-freeze to toilets
- Turn off all circuit breakers
- Disconnect battery cables

- Remove inside drain plugs in bilge
- Remove all portable electronics from cabin and bridge
- Replace summer canvases with winter covers
- Grease anchor winch on deck
- Put all deck furniture in cabin
- Polish all outside stainless steal
- Spray all bridge wire panels with preventive-spray
- In drydock open all seacocks to drain remaining salt water
- In drydock replace zincs on shafts and aft
- In drydock check that salt water intakes are clean
- Spray all salt water intakes with barnacle paint

Of course, I only use nontoxic antifreeze in all the winter applications.

After performing all the listed maintenance with tears in my eyes, I begin checking my *Spring Maintenance Schedule Checklist* for any chores that I can perform over the winter months. The schedule follows:

Spring Schedule Maintenance Checklist

- Give *Mikara* a hug and kiss
- Check outside of boat for any winter damage
- Connect Battery Cables and use protective spray
- Check lead acid battery levels
- Turn on circuit breakers
- Plug in dockside power
- Make sure battery charger is working
- Replace winter covers with summer canvases
- Remove shower caps from engines
- Replace hot water-heater by-pass plug
- Check that all fresh water systems are operational
- Open fuel valves and check for fuel leaks

- Check coolant and oil levels in engines
- Check transmission fluid levels
- Make sure all raw-water intakes are open
- Check engine hoses and replace brittle ones
- Tighten all clamps and wire connections in bilge
- Start port and starboard engines & check exhaust water flow
- Start generator and check exhaust water flow
- Start A/C unit and check water flow
- Check for hose leaks while each motor is running
- Clean & spray electronic connections
- Attach electronics and test each one
- Check anchor winch

CHAPTER SIX

BoatUS Membership, Insurance, & Towing Coverage

BoatUS Membership

I've been a member of BoatUS for over 20 years. In addition to their comprehensive boat insurance, they have benefits that cover great discounts for products and marina dockage, an impeccable towing service, a strong boating representation voice, and a great program for boating safety. The annual fee is $24, with a generous discount if you are a member of the United States Power Squadron, U.S. Coast Guard Auxiliary, and many other organizations.

For those not familiar with BoatUS, the following brief information was taken from their enormous website:

> BoatUS – Boat Owners Association of the United States – is the oldest and largest Membership association of boaters. We pride ourselves in offering service, savings, and representation since 1966.

Today, we represent over half a million Members. There is strength in our numbers, and our hands-on approach ensures that with any of our services – you always get more than what you pay for!

Membership Includes:

- 24/7 Towing Dispatch to over 600 towboats in 300+ports
- Roadside Assistance while trailering you boat
- Discounts on fuel, transient slips, repairs and more at 1,000+boating businesses
- 6 Issues of the award-winning BoatUS Magazine
- Access to Boat Insurance from dedicated experts
- The boater's advocate – from local issues to Capitol Hill
- Highest level of shopping rewards at West Marine
- Travel discounts from Star Clipper, The Moorings and more
- Discounts on Custom Boat Lettering and Registration Numbers

Membership Options:

1. Basic Membership - $24/year
2. Unlimited Saltwater Towing - $149/year
3. Unlimited Freshwater towing - $72/year

Insurance

There are any number of insurance companies that provide boat insurance. After being a paying customer of a few over my many years in boating, the best that I think is boater-friendly is purchased through BoatUS. Currently, they are using GEICO Insurance Co. I was pleasantly surprised when they gave me a generous discount for having other insurance coverage with them. For details of their coverage go to www.boatus.com/insurance.

CHAPTER SEVEN

Proper Boat Tools

Marine Tool Kit

I have been fortunate that, over the years, I had Captain Charlie buying and guiding me in the use of tools that were necessary on my boats. You might say that my tools are just the right ones needed to handle the many maintenance and repair jobs that I tackled. Each tool was purchased as needed, especially in the earlier years when there were few local marine supply stores. But today, thanks to supply outlets such as West Marine, there are many tool kits available for boats of every size and description. Some of the common tools that can be found in a handy tool kit are:

- 3/8"drive ratchet handle
- 3/8" drive x 3" extension
- 3/8"-1/4" drive adapter
- 5/8" spark plug socket
- 1- SAE and metric wrenches
- Sixteen 3/8" drive SAE and metric socket set
- Twenty-four ¼" drive SAE and metric sockets
- Metric bit driver

- 50 driver bits
- 5 driver bit holders
- 6 SAE and metric hex keys
- 2 hex key holders
- #2x4 Phillips screwdriver
- ¼"x4 slotted screwdriver
- 8" adjustable wrench
- 6" slip joint pliers
- Wire strippers/crimper

In addition to the general marine tools in a kit, I've accumulated many others, acquired over the years, such as:

- A hammer
- Different sized pliers
- Locking pliers
- Different sized screwdrivers
- A couple of monkey wrenches
- Engine tune-up kit
- Gas filter wrench
- Oil filter wrench
- Grease gun

The list can go on and on. I'm sure that each Captain will purchase the proper tools that can be used to handle the maintenance and repair work on their boats, for whatever tasks requiring their attention as they become familiar with the workings of their crafts.

CHAPTER EIGHT

Summary of Savings

In addition to the amount of cash listed below that I saved by doing preventive maintenance on my boats, I also saved tens-of-thousands of dollars on repairs and maintenance for work done as the occasion called for.

Work Done	Page	Savings
Changing Oil & Filters	9	$15,000
Winterizing Engines & A/C Units	11	20,000
Winterizing Fresh Water Systems	11	15,000
Servicing Intake Strainers	12	15,000
Engine Tune-ups Including Gas Filters & Belts	20	30,000
Replacing Zincs in Engines, Shafts, etc,	24	30,000
Waxing Boat & Hardware	25	25,000

Total		$150,000

I hope that my experience and savings will encourage captains to get involved with the repairs and maintenance of their boats. Being a pencil-pusher, I never thought that handling many of the chores on my boats would make me enjoy boating more than I could ever have imagined.

An added bonus for hands-on captains is the confidence they will have in knowing that, in case of a breakdown or an emergency, they will have a good understanding of how to handle most unexpected problems on their crafts.

LOTS OF LUCK AND HAPPY BOATING

Printed in the United States
by Baker & Taylor Publisher Services